This Journal Belongs To

_____

I AM AWESOME!

How are you awesome? Do you think that in order to be awesome that you have to be a straight "A" student or that you have to be the absolute best at basketball, playing an instrument, Minecraft® or playing chess? Nope. That's so not the case. Guess what?... EVERYBODY is awesome in some way! Here is what some kids said when asked, "How are you awesome?"

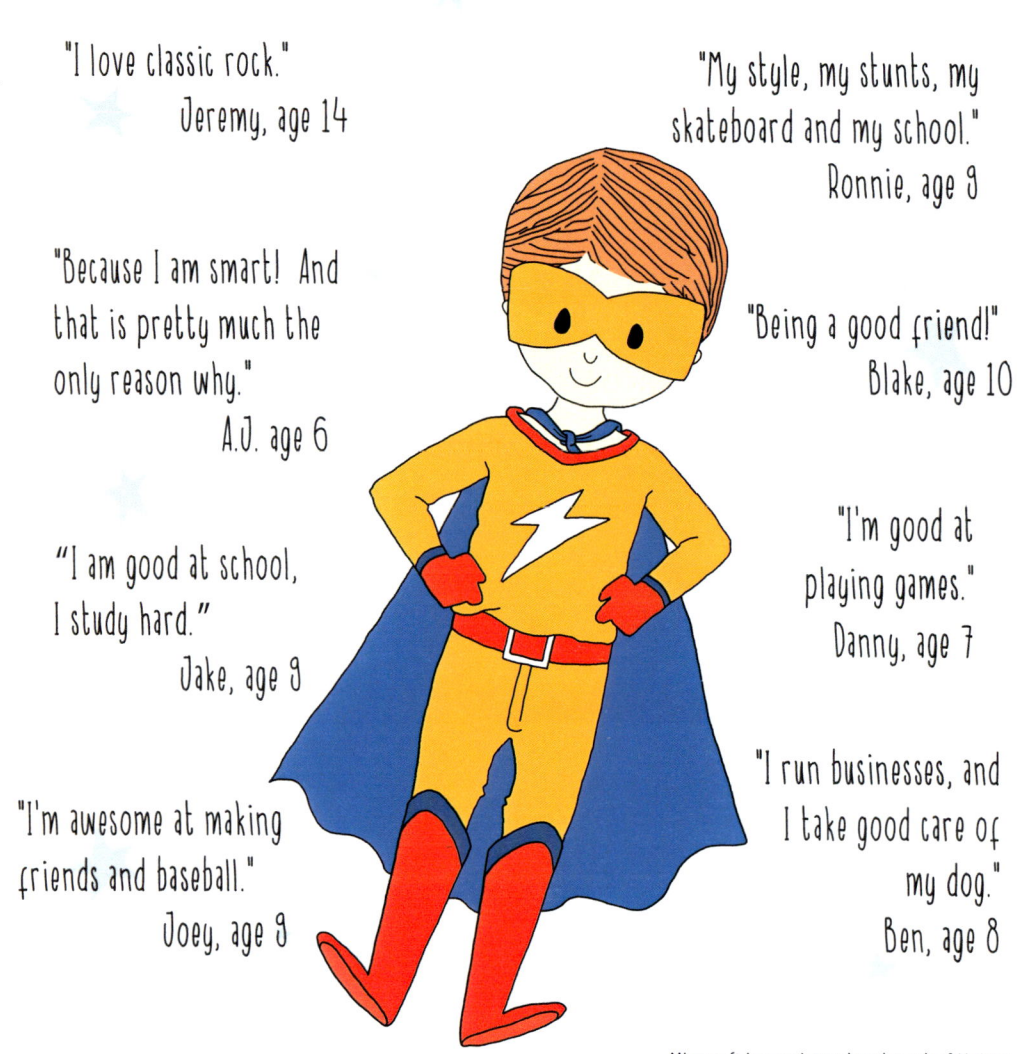

"I love classic rock."
Jeremy, age 14

"Because I am smart! And that is pretty much the only reason why."
A.J. age 6

"I am good at school, I study hard."
Jake, age 9

"I'm awesome at making friends and baseball."
Joey, age 9

"My style, my stunts, my skateboard and my school."
Ronnie, age 9

"Being a good friend!"
Blake, age 10

"I'm good at playing games."
Danny, age 7

"I run businesses, and I take good care of my dog."
Ben, age 8

Minecraft is a registered trademark of Mojang Synergies AB, a subsidiary of Microsoft.

HOW I AM AWESOME

Think about how you are awesome. Describe a time that you used your awesomeness and how you felt in that moment.

MY SUPER KID ANTHEM

An anthem is a song of celebration. You are probably familiar with the United States' national anthem, the *Star Spangled Banner*. The lyrics include words such as "proudly" and "brave." When heard, anthems often fill listeners with a sense of joy, pride and strength.

Select a song to be your anthem. Think of songs by your favorite recording artists.

Name of recording artist _____

Name of song _____

Lyrics from this song that make you feel awesome

_____
_____
_____

Why do these lyrics make you feel strong?

_____
_____
_____

LETTER TO ME

Write a letter to yourself describing the things that you appreciate and love most about you. Talk about how your supposed "flaws" are not flaws at all, but make you unique and give you strength.

Dear Me,

_____
_____
_____
_____
_____
_____
_____
_____
_____
_____
_____
_____

Sincerely,

Me

MY GOOF-UPS

Even awesome boys goof up on occasion. List your top 4 most embarrassing or goofy moments.

I KINDA GOOFED UP WHEN...

I KINDA GOOFED UP WHEN...

OOPS!

OOPS!

I KINDA GOOFED UP WHEN...

I KINDA GOOFED UP WHEN...

OOPS!

OOPS!

Now take a moment to laugh at yourself. Then move on!

SPEAK YOUR MIND!

Use this page to write about anything that has been on your mind.

ISAIAH DID IT!

When Isaiah was 9 years old, he participated in a program at Brooks Elementary School called Cool Cat Café. During Cool Cat Café students performed original works of art.

From a very early age, Isaiah enjoyed writing and illustrating books. "I liked reading graphic novels and was fascinated by the pictures," said Isaiah. "So writing my own books and drawing pictures was my way of being creative."

But Isaiah did not want to participate because performing in front of an audience scared him. However, after encouragement from his mom and dad, Isaiah agreed to participate.

The name of his book was *Chewy, the Friendly Gummi Bear*. It was all about a town of gummi bears that was terrorized by humans. The humans loved to capture the gummi bears and eat them.

On performance night, Isaiah felt nervous. However, he knew he had to do it. With his black beret and shades, Isaiah slowly walked to the stage and started to read his book. He spoke loudly and clearly. He was dramatic. He giggled as he read the funny parts. The parents, teachers and kids in the audience listened intently, curious to learn the fate of the gummi bears. They laughed throughout. When Isaiah finished, the audience jumped up and gave him a standing ovation!

Isaiah felt good about his performance at Cool Cat Café. He was happy that he overcame his fear and shared with the audience the story of Chewy and his gummi bear friends.

MY STANDING OVATION

Think about the times when you did something even though you were scared. Just like Isaiah, you deserve a standing ovation for your accomplishments.

YAY!! I deserve a standing ovation because even though I was scared, I...

_____

_____

_____

YIPPEE! I deserve a standing ovation because even though I was scared, I...

_____

_____

_____

YES!! I deserve a standing ovation because even though I was scared, I...

_____

_____

KEEP ON!

Some people say or do things that make you feel good. Their encouragement builds your confidence and makes you smile. You want them to **KEEP ON** doing or saying these types of things.

I like it when my parents

_____
_____
_____
_____

SO KEEP ON!

I like it when my teacher

_____
_____
_____
_____

SO KEEP ON!

I like it when my friend,

_____,
_____
_____
_____

SO KEEP ON!

I like it when my friend,

_____,
_____
_____
_____

SO KEEP ON!

HE HAS BOY POWER!

Homework and sports, chores and dinner,
The life of a boy, training to be a winner.
He works hard at school, excels at reading and math,
Then returns home to walk the dog and give it a bath.
He cleans up his room and plays with his brother.
He always tries to help his father and mother.
He's true to his word and his family is proud,
Of a boy who's polite and stands out in a crowd.
These are the super powers that create a true star,
This boy is awesome and his values will take him far!

JACK and BART

Jack wasn't like other kids. His way of thinking was always a little different. While his classmates were busy playing at the train table, Jack was wondering about how fast real trains could move. After school while the other kids played football at the playground, Jack would stay home and memorize statistics about the top NFL players. Jack was always interested in learning the details about the things his classmates were doing and memorized facts easily.

Jack acted differently in other ways. His classmates thought that he talked funny, walked funny, and didn't play games the way he was supposed to. Jack had a hard time making friends.

When Mrs. Hill introduced Bart the guinea pig as the new class pet, she told the class that they would share the work of taking care of their new friend. She said during silent reading time they would get to take turns holding Bart.

"Mrs. Hill!" called Isaac. "What about Jack? He isn't allowed to hold Bart, is he? What if he doesn't hold him right? He never does anything the right way."

Mrs. Hill put her hands on her hips. "Isaac, that's enough!" she scolded. "Jack is very capable of doing anything you can do." With thirty minutes until the dismissal bell, every student got a chance to hold Bart before they left school that day.

JACK and BART

That night when Jack got home from school, he asked his mother if he could read about guinea pigs on the internet. He spent a long time learning all about them. He wanted to be the very best guinea pig caretaker that he could.

The next day when the students arrived at class, Mrs. Hill had some sad news. After everyone took turns holding Bart, someone forgot to shut his cage door. He was missing!

All the kids began arguing about who left the cage door open- all except Jack. He knew exactly where Bart would be. When Jack was reading about guinea pigs on the internet, he learned that they like to hide in dark places, especially when they are nervous. All the noise of the students arguing was probably very scary to him.

"Shhhh!" he said to his classmates as he pointed to the bookcase. "Check under it!"

Mrs. Hill walked to the book case and dropped to her knees, peering underneath. She turned back to the class and smiled.

"Thank you, Jack," she said as she picked up Bart and carried him back to his cage. "I knew you'd be a great friend to Bart!" Isaac and Jack's other classmates all cheered for Jack and patted him on the back. Jack felt good that he was able to find Bart and save the day.

COLOR ME!

DREAM BIG

Write down your dreams.

MY DREAMS

What is your dream job?

What would you love to do in the future?

What is a goal you want to achieve?

Who would like to meet?

How do you want to use your awesomeness?

Who do you want to help?

Where do want to travel someday?

17

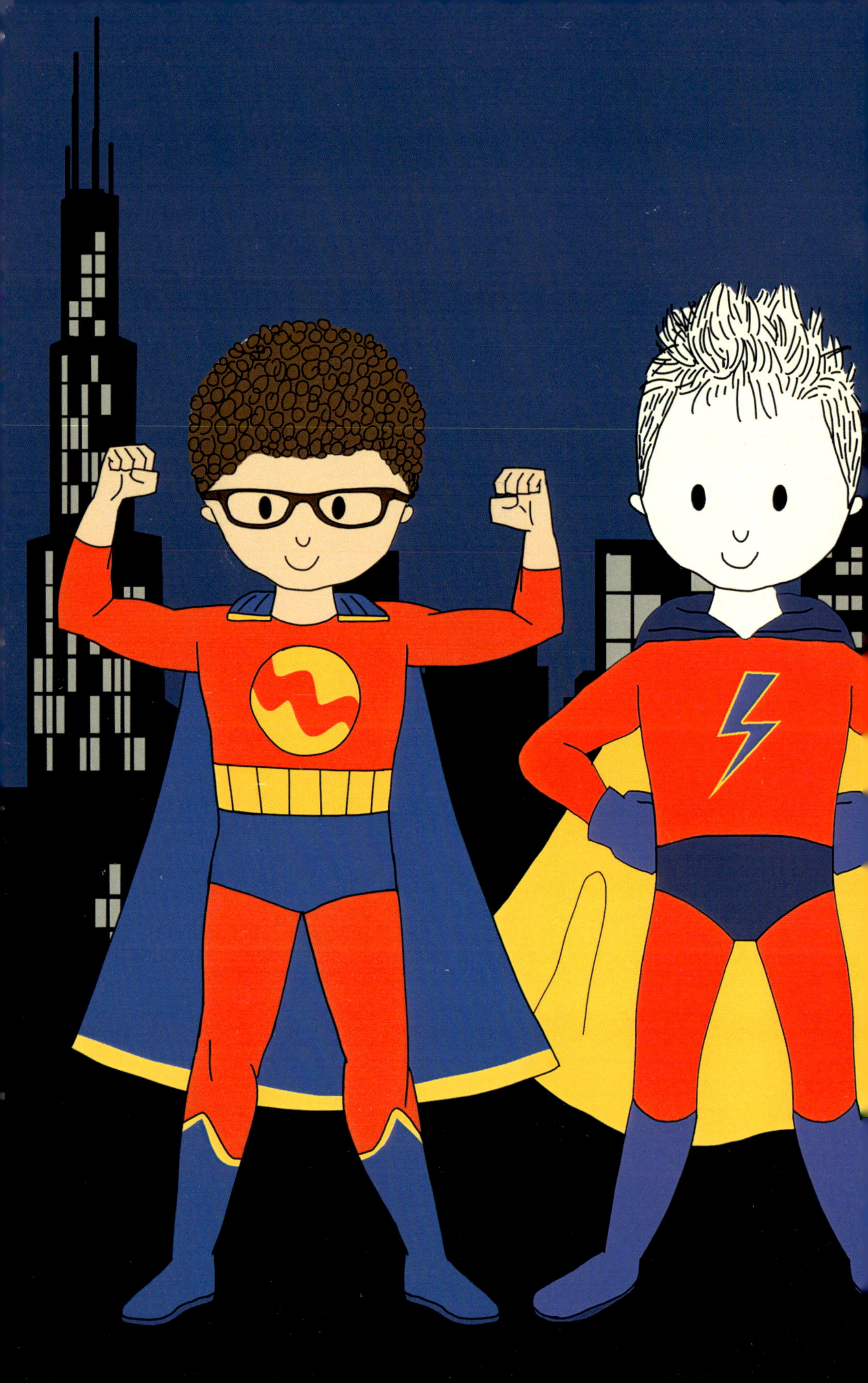

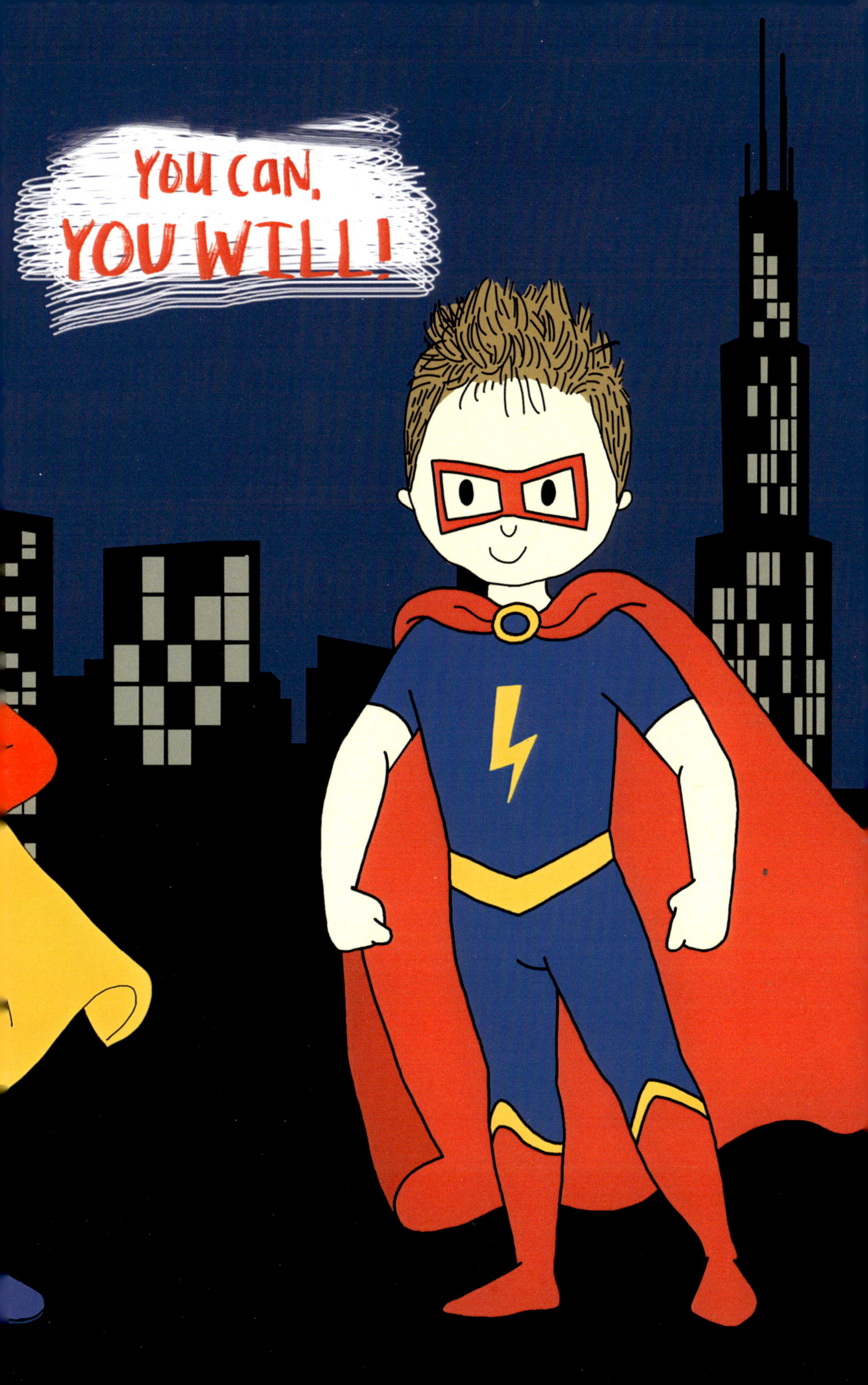
YOU CAN,
YOU WILL!

JUST STOP!

Some people say or do things that make you feel bad. They make you feel unsure of yourself and question your awesomeness. This is really annoying. You really wish they would just **STOP**!

I don't like it when my parents
_____
_____
_____
_____

SO JUST STOP!

I don't like it when my teacher
_____
_____
_____
_____

SO JUST STOP!

I don't like it when my friend,
_____,
_____
_____
_____

SO JUST STOP!

I don't like it when my friend,
_____,
_____
_____
_____

SO JUST STOP!

SPEAK YOUR MIND!

Use this page to write about *anything* that has been on your mind.

MY FAVES

Write down your favorite things.

Animal _____

Cartoon Character _____

Color _____

Book _____

Hobby _____

Movie _____

Museum _____

Place to Travel _____

Snack _____

Song _____

Sport _____

Sports Team _____

Store _____

Subject at school _____

Video game _____

DOODLE MY FAVES

Take all of the faves you listed on the previous page and write them in these letters. Use swirls, circles, and other decorations inside the letters. Draw pictures around the words. Use your creativity to complete your work of art.

MY
FAVES

SHARE YOUR AWESOMENESS

let your

VOICE

BE HEARD!

I WILL BE HEARD!

Describe a time when you were too scared or embarrassed to share your thoughts or ideas. What made you feel scared? How could you handle this type of situation differently in the future?

_____

_____

_____

_____

_____

_____

_____

_____

_____

_____

_____

_____

_____

_____

Remember: Do not be shy about sharing your awesomeness!

EVERYTHING ME

Describe yourself in great detail using only POSITIVE words. Describe your appearance, your personality, the way you like to dress including your favorite shoes, your hobbies, your likes, and your dislikes. This is a place to write down everything about you!

PORTRAIT OF ME

Now draw you! Make sure to include your favorite shirt that you like to wear or any gear you use for sports, hobbies or gaming. If you have a dog, cat, rabbit, guinea pig, or other pet that you love, include that in your picture.

MY CREW

Friends are important. Your friends laugh with you, support you, keep your secrets, and help you be the best you can be.

My good friends are _____

_____

_____

The things I look for in friends are _____

_____

_____

I am a great friend because _____

_____

_____

One thing I would never do to a friend is _____

_____

_____

Sometimes friendships can be hard because _____

_____

BE DARING!

Sometimes our fears keep us from doing things that we really want to do or things that we really should do.

Write about an occasion when your fears got the best of you.

_____

_____

_____

_____

_____

Now write about how you can put aside your fears and try something new.

_____

_____

_____

_____

_____

_____

I WISH

If you could be granted three wishes what would they be?

LETTER TO BULLY

Write a letter to someone who bullied you, hurt your feelings, or was mean to you. Explain to that person how he or she made you feel. Then set that person straight by explaining how wrong he or she was.

Dear Bully,

_____
_____
_____
_____
_____
_____
_____
_____
_____
_____
_____
_____

Sincerely,

YEP, I AM LOVED

You are loved! You are loved by more people than you may realize. Think about all of the people who care about you -- your parents, grandparents, siblings, other family members, and your friends. Even your furry buddies love you! Use this space to list all of the people who love you.

SPEAK YOUR MIND!

Use this page to write about **anything** that has been on your mind.

FEELING ANGRY OR SAD?

Everybody has moments when they do not feel that their super powers are enough. Write about a time when you felt **angry** or **sad**.

_____

_____

_____

_____

_____

Now let's flip the script. List 5 things that always make you feel **happy**--even when you are down.

1. _____

2. _____

3. _____

4. _____

5. _____

34